LIVING LIFE FROM WITHIN

LIVING LIFE FROM WITHIN

HOW TO GET WHAT YOU WANT IN LIFE

KATRINA JOHNSON

Living Life From Within
How To Get What You Want in Life

All rights reserved
Copyright © 2024 by Katrina Johnson

No part of this publication may be reproduced, distributed, or transmitted in any form or by any means, including photocopying, recording, or other electronic or mechanical methods, without the prior written permission of the publisher, except in the case of brief quotations embodied in critical reviews and certain other noncommercial uses permitted by copyright law.

Published by Spines
ISBN: 979-8-89383-005-7

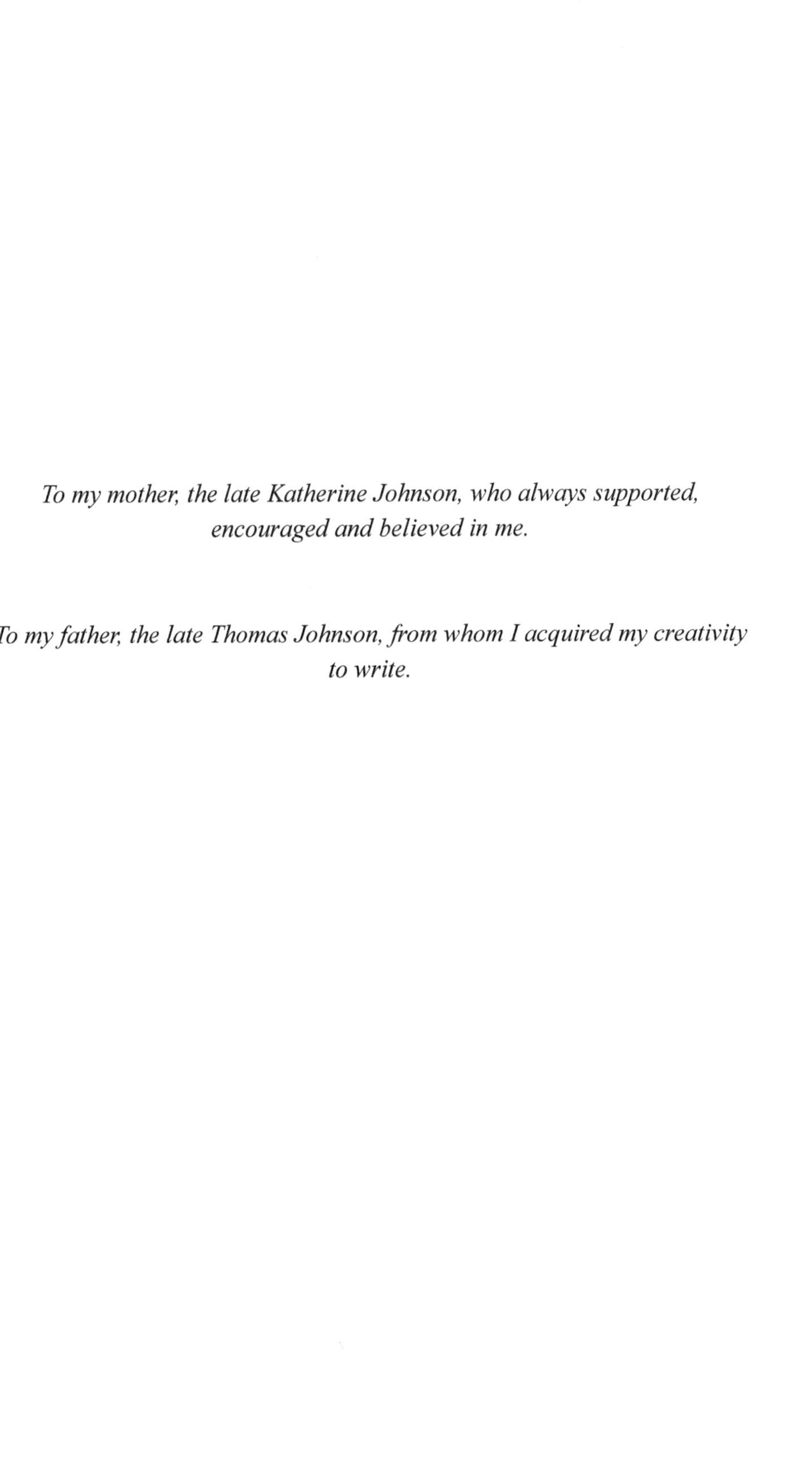

To my mother, the late Katherine Johnson, who always supported, encouraged and believed in me.

To my father, the late Thomas Johnson, from whom I acquired my creativity to write.

CONTENTS

ACKNOWLEDGMENTS

I want to acknowledge some people who were there and witnessed my life trajectory first-hand in 2016. To my children who love, support, and encourage me daily., my unconditional love for you all is everlasting.

Victoria, you don't know how much you helped Mommy get through one of the roughest times in my life.

My sister Cynthia, thank you for being my sounding board at a time when I could not think clearly. Your patience in listening to me cry my heart out means more to me than you may ever know. Love you, Sis!

My dear friend Laura, who has a heart of gold, I don't know what I would have done without your kindness, generosity, and support when I needed it the most. Love you girl!

FOREWORD

It is with great pleasure and admiration that I write this foreword for my dear friend, Katrina Johnson. I had the privilege of meeting Katrina three years ago at a Toastmasters meeting, and from the moment I heard her speak, I knew she was destined for greatness. In "Living Life From Within: How to Get What You Want in Life," Katrina shares her remarkable story of resilience, determination, and personal growth. Through her words, she takes us on a transformative journey, inviting us to reflect on our own lives and discover the untapped potential within us.

Katrina's journey is one of triumph over adversity. She faced numerous challenges and setbacks, but instead of succumbing to defeat, she found the strength to rise above them. Her unwavering belief in herself and her ability to overcome obstacles is truly inspiring. Through her involvement in Toastmasters, Katrina honed her public speaking skills and discovered her passion for empowering others. She became a beacon of light, guiding individuals on their paths to self-discovery and personal growth. Her ability to connect with people on a deep level is a testament to her authenticity and genuine desire to make a difference.

"Living Life From Within: How to Get What You Want in Life" is not just a book; it is a roadmap for personal transformation. Katrina's insights, wisdom, and practical advice will empower readers to embrace their true potential and live a life of purpose and fulfillment. Her words will resonate with anyone who has ever felt stuck, lost, or unsure of their path.   As I reflect on the impact Katrina has had on my life and the lives of countless others, I am reminded of the power of human connection and the profound influence one person can have.

I am honored to call Katrina my friend, and I am grateful for the opportunity to witness her growth and evolution over the years. Her book, "Living Life From Within: How to Get What You Want in Life," is a testament to her unwavering commitment to helping others unleash their full potential. I do not doubt that this book will touch the hearts and minds of readers around the world, inspiring them while on their path to self-improvement.

It is my sincere hope that you find as much inspiration and guidance in these pages as I have. Congratulations, Katrina, on this remarkable achievement. May your words continue to inspire and empower others for years to come.

Warmest regards,

Shirley Allen

Master Trainer

Affinity Real Estate & Mortgage Training Services

Mlotrainingacademy.com

800-991-6097 x 2

PREFACE

"**Don't let the noise of other's opinions drown out your own inner voice**"

~ **Steve Jobs**

This book is designed to fuel your inner spirit and ambitions so that you may overcome challenges and get to where you can live life at a higher level.

Whether you're seeking motivation for personal growth, professional success, or simply a daily dose of positivity, let the quotes and messages empower you to reach new heights and embrace the limitless possibilities that lie ahead.

What we think and the emotions we harbor, in addition to our actions or the lack thereof, produce the circumstances in our lives. It is true that our ability to think in a way that produces good or unfavorable life experiences is based on our thought processes. Hence, what we think about begins the process of answered prayers/manifestations and how we choose to do life.

From a spiritual, philosophical point of view, according to the French philosopher Pierre Teilhard de Chardin, "We are not human beings having a spiritual experience; we are spiritual beings having a human experience."

When I first heard this perspective, it resonated with me, and I sum it up as follows: I was first created in the spiritual realm, which is the unseen realm, before coming on the scene as a human being on this earthly journey.

In other words, I know that my existence is based on something greater than what the eyes can see, and that is being spirit first and foremost.

We all live from within, whether we realize it or not. If you have bitterness inside of you, that's what will come out of you. If you have joy, peace, happiness, and love in your heart, that is what you will demonstrate outwardly. However, we are not always aware that sometimes, we just need to be still, be silent, and hear from God. God's timing and plans can't be matched. But we can stop the flow when we don't do our part.

What is our part? Our part is to follow the inner voice/spirit/God/intuition, whichever way you choose to refer to it; do know that it is a God-given gift.

For this book, I may refer to it interchangeably with all of the above phrases.

We miss hearing the inner voice when we are too busy focusing on other things. The inner voice is always speaking to us, but we are so preoccupied that we forget to listen. Many times, I walk out the door, and the inner voice tells me that I forgot something. I turn around and head back to get what I forgot, which is usually instantaneously revealed to me. Is this familiar in your life, too? We may not always know our next move, but God does. Our job is not to miss hearing that inner voice and to follow through by taking action.

We all have the power to do great things. We need to first know this, without a shadow of a doubt, and second, we should never forget it. The inner voice is the one thing that we can count on, but it's often overlooked. It's that knowing that we somehow know something is to be or that something isn't right. Oftentimes, we reason it away, and in reasoning, we may make wrong decisions, which may take us off course, delay us, or set us back.

When this happens, think of it as a lesson. Know that we can get back on track, and we will have many more opportunities to exercise the gift of the inner voice in our life situations. Look at it as a part of our journey to learn how to incorporate living from within not only to receive tangibly the things that we desire but also in a way that guides us daily.

I pray that everyone knows God as their supply source in all things. Also, they follow the leading of the inner voice and learn to pray with a deep desire to manifest what they want in life. Ultimately, may this book bless, inform, inspire, and transform the lives of everyone who reads it.

Disclaimer

I am not telling you how to think; rather, I am sharing with you my thoughts on how to make a better life for yourself based on my own life experiences.

The goal is to make you aware of the most valuable and important thing that you have inside of yourself: the spirit that is within you and the power of your subconscious mind.

The connection of both is what is important to achieve and get anything you want in your life. After reading this book, you choose what you want to think and do. The choice is yours.

1

CONQUER YOUR FEARS AND BELIEVE IN YOURSELF

"Fears are nothing more than a state of mind"

~ Napoleon Hill

If I had allowed fear to control me, and believe me, it did have its way with me for a while, this book would not have been written. Nor would I have experienced the journey toward a better life. Living life from within is to be led by the spirit that lives within us. Fear can block our ability to live from within as it will make us think the opposite of what is real. When you feel fear, know that it is only a feeling. It doesn't have to control you. You can choose to advance, despite it.

Each time you face your fears, you get bolder as you build your confidence. Over time, you will see that it becomes easier to face fear head-on. So don't give up on your dreams because of fear. Instead, use fear as your motivation to keep moving forward. Remember, the greater the risk, the greater the reward. Believe in yourself enough to know that you can overcome anything that stands in your way. I encourage you to go ahead and conquer your fears!

Most people have no idea of their potential. They don't realize that they are capable of much more than they think. We are all equipped with the ability to achieve great things, but we often limit ourselves by our own beliefs.

It's great to have people who believe in you and what you aspire to do. It is more important to believe in yourself, especially when others may not. When you live your life from within, you will find that you are capable of achieving more than you ever thought possible. You have the power to do great things and to make a difference in the world, but you have to believe in yourself; you have to be willing to work hard and take risks.

Don't let anyone tell you that you can't succeed. There is nothing that can hold you back except your own self-doubt and fear, which we already know we must face in order to overcome. It's time for you to rise above those negative emotions and start believing in yourself. Utilize the God-given power that is within you to live your life on your terms.

When you do that, anything is possible. You can achieve anything you set your mind to. Don't shy away from taking the necessary steps to move forward in life. You may just surprise yourself with what you're able to accomplish.

Remember, if you want to achieve more in life, you need to start by believing in yourself. You need to believe that you are capable of more than you currently believe. You need to start thinking big and picturing yourself achieving great things. You can do it!

2

CONNECTING THE DOTS

"If you don't like something, change it. If you can't change it, change your attitude"

~ Maya Angelou

U p until recently, I had often struggled with what my purpose was in life, not knowing that I was living it all along. What I learned after dedicating my life to God in the early 1980s is that I was to serve and worship Him. But the missing component was that I wasn't serving and worshiping Him with my gift. Giving people words of encouragement to overcome obstacles and live their best lives is something that not only comes easily to me but also lights up my soul.

However, I wasn't connecting the dots. Eventually, it all came together when I realized that my gift was to uplift others by way of writing and speaking in ways of encouragement. I now know that inspirational speaking and writing is the gift with which I worship and serve God when I uplift the lives of others.

After falling asleep one night during the first week of May 2022, meditating on these words; "God is my source," God woke me the next morning with the title of this book that you are now reading. What does it mean to live life from within? Living life from within is that gut feeling you get. It's that thing that is compelling you to do or not do something. It's intuition, that inner voice; it is when you are being spirit-led. Ultimately, it is allowing God, who is your source, to lead you and guide you on this earth plane.

In life, we can live from within. Unfortunately, we miss the mark more times than not. Additionally, living life from within is knowing how to pray with the deepest desire to manifest what you want. The opportunity to tap into the power inside of us is golden.

One thing that I discovered along my journey to live my best life was that I had no one to blame for where I was in life but myself. What I also recognized was that relationships played an intricate part in not living my best life. The reason why I say this is because, in relationships, we have to compromise, we sometimes lose focus on our goals, and perhaps our intentions may be to fill a void in our own lives. The need to be whole and content before we commit to a relationship is what a lot of people fail to realize. I can truly say that I would have benefited from starting my self-improvement journey earlier in life and before getting involved in a relationship or before marriage, for that matter.

In 2016, I discovered what it means to live life from within when I realized that the marriage I was in at the time was no longer serving me. It was my second marriage, and deciding to remove myself from the union of that marriage was the beginning of my regaining my self-esteem and making a better life for myself a priority. It was during that time that I miraculously received the manifestation of what I had prayed for.

An attempt to move to another state with my ex-husband and two younger children backfired. When I say backfired, we had packed up and driven across the country just to revert to where we were moving from in less than a month. Back at square one, without a job, no vehicle, no place to live, and some personal items that were purposely left in storage to be transported later, it would take a miracle for me to venture out on my own.

Let me share how I was able to use my faith and discover what it means to live life from within and manifest at God's speed. First, something happened when I made up my mind to remove myself from the marriage. There was a definite shift in my thinking. You might say that the fight or flight response kicked in due to the life stressors that I was under, which were further triggered by events during that road trip period. I decided to flee. Nothing was more pressing on me than coming up with a plan to change the trajectory of my life. Even to the point of hitting, what to me was rock bottom.

I did not like the position my life was in or the direction it was going. I knew I had to do something about it. It took a lot of courage and faith to make a major life-changing decision when I had nothing but God to depend on. While driving back across the country, I remember praying with great intensity and with a deep desire for a place to stay, a car, a job, and to be able to get my belongings out of storage. It was probably after midnight when we arrived back home (the place of our original departure.) We slept overnight at our daughter's place.

When morning came, I knew exactly what to do. It was as if the instructions came to me overnight. I wasted no time. I contacted three people to secure a place for me to live and a place to store my belongings that I was to get out of storage. The first phone call I made was to someone I knew who owned a house that was vacant before we left town to travel across the country. I asked if she would mind renting out one of her rooms to me. Unfortunately, she had just rented the property. The next call was to a lady that I had befriended at the last church we had attended. I asked if she knew of anyone who might have a room for rent. She did not have anyone she could refer me to who could help me in my predicament. My third and last call was to a good friend. Ironically, I did not ask her for a place to stay. I knew that she had a rather large garage, so I asked if she would allow me to store my storage items in her garage. I briefly shared my situation with her, and what happened next was nothing less than miraculous.

My friend has one of the biggest hearts that I know. She not only told me I could put my things in her garage but informed me that a co-worker had just moved out of her spare bedroom and offered it to me, and on top of that, she said if I needed a car, I could use her spare vehicle. Now, that is what I call living life from within and getting what you want in life. Ultimately, it's how we should always live life.

I saw that experience as changing for the better, which refers to the process of making positive transformations in various aspects of life, including personal development, behavior, habits, relationships, and overall well-being. It involves recognizing areas for improvement, setting goals, and taking deliberate actions to create a more fulfilling and purposeful life.

One of the key motivations for changing for the better is the desire for personal growth and self-improvement. It requires us to engage in self-reflection, identify areas of our lives that are not aligned with our values or aspirations, and take proactive steps to make positive changes. This can involve addressing negative habits, limiting beliefs, or unhealthy patterns of behavior and replacing them with healthier alternatives.

Changing for the better often involves breaking free from comfort zones and embracing new challenges. It requires us to be open to learning, exploring new possibilities, and taking risks. By stepping outside of familiar routines and environments, we can expand our horizons, discover hidden talents and passions, and unlock our full potential.

Furthermore, changing for the better often involves developing and cultivating positive habits and routines. This can include adopting healthy lifestyle choices such as regular exercise, balanced nutrition, quality sleep, and stress management techniques. It may also involve enhancing skills, acquiring knowledge, and seeking personal or professional development opportunities.

Changing for the better can also have a significant impact on relationships. It may involve improving communication skills, practicing empathy and understanding, and fostering healthier and more meaningful connections with others. By working on ourselves, we can create positive ripple effects in our interactions with family, friends, colleagues, and the broader community.

It is important to note that changing for the better is a gradual process that requires patience, perseverance, and self-compassion. It is common to encounter setbacks or face resistance along the way. However, viewing these obstacles as learning opportunities and maintaining a growth mindset can help us stay motivated and continue on our path of positive change.

Moreover, changing for the better is not a one-time event but an ongoing journey. As we evolve and grow, new opportunities for improvement and growth may arise. Embracing a mindset of continuous learning and self-improvement allows us to adapt to changing circumstances, embrace new challenges, and continue evolving into the best versions of ourselves.

If you're ready for a transformative process that involves personal growth, self-reflection, and taking deliberate actions to create a more fulfilling and purposeful life, you will need to overcome fear and embrace change. By addressing areas for improvement, embracing new challenges, cultivating positive habits, and fostering meaningful relationships, you can experience profound positive changes and create a life that aligns with your values and aspirations.

3

CONSCIOUS MIND

"The Conscious mind is your thinking mind You can accept or reject any idea here"

~ Bob Proctor

Our conscious mind is a vital aspect of our overall cognitive functioning and is responsible for our awareness, perception, thoughts, and decision-making processes. It is the part of our mind that we actively experience and engage with daily.

The conscious mind is often described as the "tip of the iceberg" because it represents only a small fraction of our total mental activity. It is the part of our mind that we are aware of at any given moment. We use our conscious mind to process sensory information from our environment, engage in logical thinking, and make conscious choices and decisions.

One of the primary functions of the conscious mind is perception. It allows us to receive and interpret information from our senses, such as sight, hearing, taste, smell, and touch. Through perception, we construct our subjective reality and make sense of the world around us.

The conscious mind is also where our thoughts arise. It is the thinking, analyzing, and problem-solving part of our mind. We use our conscious mind to process information, generate ideas, plan and strategize, and engage in logical reasoning. Our conscious thoughts can range from mundane everyday considerations to complex conceptualizations and abstract thinking.

Additionally, the conscious mind plays a crucial role in decision-making. It evaluates options, weighs pros and cons, considers consequences, and selects a course of action. Decision-making involves both rational thinking and emotional factors, and the conscious mind integrates these various aspects to arrive at a decision.

However, it is important to note that the conscious mind has limitations. It has a limited capacity for information processing, and we can only consciously focus on a limited number of thoughts or stimuli at a given time. This is why we often rely on automatic and subconscious processes to handle routine tasks and behaviors, freeing up conscious resources for more complex activities.

I spent years setting myself up for failure unconsciously, and now I'm consciously working on setting myself up for success. I've learned that what I think about matters a great deal in how my life is played out. I know now that I must control my thoughts in order to produce the life that I want. That decision I made in 2016 began with a conscious thought that led to a burning desire that enabled me to tap into the power within that I had never experienced at such a level.

Once you know your source, think about what you want and want it with intensity! To know my source is to have a life with no limitations. What do I mean by source? The God that lives in me. The creator of the universe, who is omnipotent (all-powerful), omnipresent (everywhere at the same time), omniscient (all-knowing). I believe that as long as I stay connected to my source, there is nothing that I can't have, do, or be. I have experienced this in my life, and I want to share this truth with you as well.

To get everything you want in life, you must first know where your source of power comes from and have a deep desire for whatever it is that you want, and you must follow up by taking action. That is what true power is! Staying connected to the source that is the creator of all. It's the same as an electrical device that must be connected to a power source in order to work. You may ask, how do I stay connected? First, you will need to know that there is a great power within you. I refer to that great power as God.

If you do not believe in God, or as some might say, a higher power, then this book may not resonate with you. But, I must say that if you've ever experienced having such a deep desire or need for something or for a change to take place in your life and received that thing or saw that change miraculously take place, then I would dare to say that you experienced tapping into your source.

Once you know that there is a great power within you, then you will have to consciously train your mind to be sensitive to hearing the inner voice, practice being intentional about deeply desiring what you want, and fortify staying connected through prayer and or meditation.

Since I've made the discovery in my life of what it means to live life from within, and because I stay connected to my source, I believe that I can have, be, and do anything I deeply desire.

4

SUBCONSCIOUS

"The Subconscious mind cannot tell the difference between what is real or imagined"

~ Bob Proctor

Beyond the conscious mind lies the vast realm of the subconscious mind. The subconscious mind encompasses and processes information that is not readily accessible to our conscious awareness but still influences our thoughts, emotions, and behaviors. The subconscious mind stores memories, beliefs, and experiences and can have a profound impact on our conscious thoughts and actions.

Keep in mind that our conscious mind is the aspect of our mind that we actively experience and engage with. It is responsible for our awareness, perception, thoughts, and decision-making processes. While the conscious mind plays a crucial role in our daily functioning, it is important to recognize that it represents only a fraction of our total mental activity, with much of our cognitive processes occurring beneath the surface in the subconscious mind.

Once I learned that the subconscious mind essentially aids in producing in life what I believe, whether true or not, I began to think in a way that brings more of what I want versus what I don't want in my life. The interesting thing is that my experience in 2016 occurred before I gained knowledge about the subconscious mind. In other words, I guess you can say I stumbled upon it out of desperation for a better life.

I had made the discovery of my life, of what it means to live life from within. The only way that I can describe it is that I put pressure on God. I was fed up with my life as it was. I wanted better. I wanted more. I figured out what it was that I didn't want and what was no longer serving me. I looked at my life and thought, how did you get here, but more than that, how are you going to get out of this?

That began my journey to living my best life. Some say living your best life is having all the material things, like being rich. That is only part of the equation. In my opinion, living your best life is being at peace and enjoying every moment while living in the moment. It is realizing where you were and how far you've come.

Living your best life is always having a grateful heart and being thankful for the things that you have and the things that you were able to overcome. I may not have all the money in the world, and as a matter of fact, I will never have all the money in the world. Truth be told, no one has all the money in the world. But one thing I do know is everything is abundant.

Money, material things, and natural resources that we see every day, like trees, green pastures, and mountains, are all in abundance. What most people don't realize is that there is no limit to the things that they can have. The only limit is the limit that they hold to themselves.

Perhaps it's time to change that narrative about limitations. Some of us were brought up to think in terms of lack because we've heard terms like money doesn't grow on trees and other negative stereotypical statements that we believe to be true. Going back to what I said about putting pressure on God because I had come to a point in my life where I was desperately in need of change, my prayer life was taken to a whole new level.

At the time, I had no idea what I was doing. All I knew was that my intentions at that point in my life were so strong that I manifested everything that I desired. When I began to experience one miracle on top of others, I asked myself, how did that happen? What was it that I did to bring forth these miracles? The only answer I could find was that I got to that point of no return. I was desperately eager and, without a shadow of a doubt, knew that I had to make a new way in life for myself.

The Bible speaks of fervent prayer in James 5:16: "The effectual fervent prayer of a righteous man availeth much." I would like to say that that is exactly what I was doing. I was praying a fervent prayer without ceasing with strong intention, and that is how I got to where I am today.

Have I reached the point where I can say I have fulfilled all of my dreams and am at the top of my game? No, but every day, I'm living my best life.

You might ask how I do it. Let me share with you some truths that I believe everyone should have access to because we are all given the same power by the Creator to have anything and everything we want. We are all given the same power to be able to create and recognize the abundance that's available to us. Sometimes, as with myself, it may take falling flat on your face or hitting the bottom pit, so to speak, before we wake up. But when you do wake up, you will realize how simple the process can be.

What I'm sharing with you about receiving what it is that you desire can sound a bit mind-blowing, but it's true, and it is available to everyone, not just a few, but every soul that lives on earth. Everyone can turn their lives around, have a better way of living, and have whatever it is they desire, in reason, meaning you can not overstep boundaries by desiring something in the way of coveting. An example would be desiring another person who may be someone else's spouse. That would be out of line. Attempting to override someone's will, to manipulate them, is not what this is about either.

One thing I've learned by being a woman of faith is that your faith matters the most. In church, I've learned that if you believe what you pray for, you can have what you pray for. It is something that's been embedded in me. However, I did not know how to apply the fervent prayer without ceasing. I used to physically, literally go into my prayer closet, and there is nothing wrong with that, to pray to God daily, pretty much on a schedule. My prayers have gotten me out of a whole lot of situations. It's gotten me through times of turmoil. God is real, and I will always be grateful to my creator. What I learned, though, is that you don't have to have a certain time of day to pray (though I make prayer the first thing I do in the morning), and you don't have to always go into your prayer closet to hear from God and to have your prayers answered.

When it comes to praying, what you need to do is get it fixed in your mind, specifically, what it is you desire. That desire, if it is deep enough, will be your fervent prayer. You must then follow up by taking some form of action. This is the blueprint for living life from within concerning having your prayers manifested. God will answer as long as you are faithful in believing that he hears you. Let me re-emphasize that the prayer in 2016 was so impressed upon my subconscious mind that I received everything I prayed for and followed with action, and it happened right away.

5

KNOWLEDGE AND UNDERSTANDING

"Once you know what failure feels like, determination chases success"

~ Kobe Bryant

I was taught scripture references in church, which I also affirmed, some being: seek, and ye shall find, knock, and the door shall be open; faith without work is dead, ask, and you shall receive, the fervent prayers of the righteous avail much, and pray without ceasing. The sad thing is that I wasn't taught how to apply the scriptures properly to live life from within and manifest my deepest desires.

Having knowledge but not having the full understanding, I could not implement the scriptures in the way where I would see manifested prayers in my life. When I started seeking to know more about God, I gained information, inspiration, and, ultimately, transformation in my life.

It was through the books that I read and various videos that broke down spirituality and its connection with science that took my life to a new level. The knowledge and understanding that I had acquired from these resources is what I had been missing in the church.

Let me explain. Imagine your mind as a powerful machine with two parts: the conscious and the subconscious. The conscious mind is like the captain of a ship, making decisions and giving orders. It's the part you're aware of, where you think and reason.

Now, think of the subconscious mind as the engine room of the ship. It's always working in the background, even when you're not paying attention. It stores all your memories, beliefs, and experiences, shaping how you see the world and how you respond to situations.

Scripture, like a guiding map, provides instructions for both your conscious and subconscious minds. When you pray, you're essentially sending a message to both parts of your mind and to a higher power, asking for guidance or help.

Here's how it all works together:

1. Conscious Mind: When you pray and focus on specific scriptures, your conscious mind is actively engaged. You're consciously choosing to believe in the words you're reading and speaking.

2. Subconscious Mind: As you repeat these prayers and scriptures, they start sinking into your subconscious mind like seeds planted in fertile soil. Your subconscious mind doesn't question or doubt; it simply accepts and acts upon the beliefs you feed it.

3. Alignment: When your conscious and subconscious minds are aligned with the teachings of scripture, they work together harmoniously to manifest your prayers. Positive affirmations from scripture resonate deeply within you, influencing your thoughts, emotions, and actions.

4. Answered Prayers: As your subconscious mind internalizes the messages from scripture, it begins to shape your reality. You may find yourself naturally gravitating towards solutions, opportunities, or people that align with

your prayers. It's like setting a course for your ship and letting the engine (your subconscious mind) propel you toward your destination.

In simpler terms, knowing how scripture interacts with your conscious and subconscious mind is like understanding how to navigate a ship using a reliable map. By aligning your thoughts and beliefs with the wisdom of scripture, you harness the power of your mind to bring your prayers to fruition.

I question why church leaders are not teaching people the Godly principles of living an abundant life based on mindset principles as they relate to our conscious and subconscious minds. I asked myself, do they not know that our conscious and subconscious minds play an integral part in what we believe and how we see ourselves?

However, the scriptures do say to study to show thyself approved. Therefore, I take full responsibility, and I can only blame myself for not seeking knowledge and understanding before I came to it.

6

———

INTENTIONS

**"You create your thoughts, your thoughts create your intentions, and
your intentions create your reality"**

~ Wayne W. Dyer

Research has revealed intention, as it pertains to philosophy, as a determination or will to create reality. I believe that being intentional with your life is, in a nutshell, growth. We grow when we intentionally make an effort to be a better person or improve in other areas of life.

Being intentional about fulfilling my purpose for existing was easy once I was ready to improve my life. Sometimes, we can get comfortable with being uncomfortable. We may believe that we have no way out of a situation and feel as though we have no choice but to remain in a stagnant position. That was me at one point in my life.

It wasn't until I became intentional with my life and took responsibility for the part that I played in allowing myself to get to the point of being fed up that I stopped being comfortable with being in an uncomfortable situation.

After giving thought to what was lacking in my life and realizing that the need for change was evident, a better life sounded good to me.

One day, I decided what I wanted, as well as what I no longer wanted in my life. I wanted stability and security. What I no longer wanted to accept was a life that was the exact opposite, one of instability and insecurity.

I was insecure about where I was physically and emotionally. Physically, I was tired of relocating from one place to the other. You see, at a point in my life during my previous marriage, we often struggled to have a place to call home. Mentally, I had lost my sense of self, and my self-esteem was at an all-time low. I began to fear that things would never improve.

I began to lose confidence in myself and the future of my family. Stability, for me, is a top priority in my life. To know that I have prepared, planned, and taken steps to secure, to the best of my ability, a lifestyle that represents a sense of predictability trumps instability without a doubt.

Since 2016, my intention has been to improve my life, and I've been doing just that, and I will continue to self-improve as long as I'm living. But I've also added something to go along with my self-improvement journey, and that is to inspire others on their self-improvement journey path.

7

SELF-IMPROVMENT

"Change you and see your circumstances change"

~ Katrina Johnson

To live life from within cannot be done if we fail to work on improving ourselves. Self-improvement takes patience, courage, determination, diligence, and willpower. It doesn't happen overnight. Every small step leads to a bigger goal. You must want it bad enough to not give in when things get tough. Remembering why you started on the path to the life that you are creating for yourself is key. We all have areas in our lives that need to be improved upon. We love the peaks in life, but when the valleys come, we are tested. The valley periods provide us with a choice to be bitter or get better.

Here is how we can begin to self-improve and better ourselves:

- We have to first make up our minds that we want to do better
- Determine what is no longer serving us or what we no longer want
- Decide on what we want
- Then, begin to execute and take the necessary steps toward self-improvement

There will be plenty of opportunities to quit, but you are not a quitter. At times, all you may need to do is adjust, recharge, and tweak some things in your life. It beats giving up hope toward your dreams and desires. Fuel the passion that's deep within. Passion is the thing that gives you wings to soar. The journey precedes the blessings.

Though we may not understand why some things happen along our journey in life, in the end, once we learn from the lessons and can appreciate the wisdom we obtain, then it will make sense, and the blessings will flow.

It may not always look like it, but life is on your side. Learn valuable lessons along the way. Be proud of how far you've come and how strong you are. You will be glad that you didn't give up on life and, ultimately, on yourself.

8

IMPOSTER SYNDROME

**"I still have a little impostor syndrome…
It doesn't go away, that feeling that you shouldn't
take me that seriously. What do I know?
I share that with you because we all have doubts
in our abilities, about our power and what that power is"**

~ Michelle Obama

In an earlier section of this book, you may recall me stating that I could have allowed fear to stop me from writing this book. After all, I had never authored a book before. Who was I to think that I could? What will people think about my book? These and other self-doubting thoughts plagued my mind, all boiling down to me having imposter syndrome.

Psychology Today explains that people who struggle with imposter syndrome believe that they are undeserving of their achievements and the high esteem in which they are, in fact, generally held. Have you experienced this? I'm sure most of us have. But we get over it by confronting fear head-on.

I always like to use the Cinderella syndrome to counteract the imposter syndrome. Cinderella syndrome says you're scared, but you do it anyway.

Another point I made at the beginning of this book was how living life from within can impact a person's life negatively or positively. Let me provide an example of what I mean by this. If I had allowed imposter syndrome to take up residence in my mind, the outcome would have been negative. The negative outcome would be based on me believing the lies from within, telling me that I was not capable.

Hence, the book you are now reading would not exist physically. However, it would exist within me trapped inside due to imposter syndrome. This is why it is so important to live life from within in a positive light because living with negative energy is just as effective as living with positive energy when it comes to manifesting.

I ask you to consider what you want. Always ask yourself, "What do I want?" That question and the answer you give will be a key factor for what you do in your life to get what you want. Unfortunately, some people will choose a negative outcome based solely on their belief that they can do no better in life. That is their choice to live life from within in such a way that they don't want to grow to their full potential. But not you; you were born to be and do more than you can imagine.

9

THE RIGHT MINDSET

"Your mindset determines the results you get in life"

~ Katrina Johnson

The right mindset has everything to do with living life from within. At the beginning of this book, I mentioned how our thoughts are key to what type of life we create for ourselves. I want to break down some mindset food for thought here.

Negativity says:

Things are bad, and that's just how it is.

Positivity says:

Good can be found in every unfavorable situation.

One thing is for sure: thoughts of negativity will never produce positive outcomes. Think, be, and live positively. We are either unaware, or we often forget, that our minds are very powerful in that we can create good and bad experiences based on what we think about.

If we don't like the way things are in the world, but all we do is complain and carry on negatively, are we part of the cause, or are we part of the solution?

It's all in how we perceive things. It boils down to mindset. It's a fixed mindset vs a growth mindset. The question is, where do you see yourself in the equation? An indecisive and uncommitted mind goes hand in hand. We cannot commit to something without first making a decision.

Here are some tips for having the right mindset that will enable you to achieve what you want in life:

- Have a vision
- Make a decision
- Commit to the mission
- Then comes the provision

It's an amazing thing that we may not always have the answers to how we will make something happen. However, once we decide to go forward with our plans, the doors of opportunity will open for us. Having the right mindset is one of the keys to a good life. The achievement will become quite effortless and miraculous.

Know that when you are building something, the completion may not happen overnight, but eventually, as long as you are steadfast, you will have a completed project. One of the biggest challenges is not allowing anything to stop your flow. If we have the right mindset, if we focus on self-improvement, and if we are truly looking to succeed and overcome obstacles, we can overcome and succeed. No matter what happens today, this week, or the rest of the year, whatever is thrown your way as an attempt to stop your flow, don't let it. You have everything within you to keep it moving, to overcome, and to succeed.

It's been said that achieving the things that we want in life takes hard work.

The most challenging part of working hard first happens in our minds.

Once our minds are in the right place, meaning the right thoughts, beliefs, intentions, and ultimately, the right mindset, there is nothing that we can not do.

Essentially, doors open, opportunities present themselves, and just like that, we can almost effortlessly get, do, and achieve what we want. We must trust the process and embrace the progress. Be the person that when others look at you and ask, how do you do what you do? Tell them it's your mindset.

To fail is to give up. Tell them that you believe in pushing yourself towards your goals and you're committed to staying on the path to the end. Live your life from within, and you will accomplish and obtain what you deeply desire.

10

CONCLUSION

"The starting point of all achievement is DESIRE"

~ Napoleon Hill

The main thing here is that you can have the things you want, do things that you would like to do, and live a fulfilling life when following certain principles:

- Believe that there is a power source (which I refer to as God) that is inside of you, waiting for you to tap in.
- Know that your thoughts, with action applied, not only are a key factor to the results that you bring into your life but also can be attributed to your mental state of mind.
- Know that a deep desire for something can become your reality when you have fervently prayed/impressed that deep desire upon your subconscious mind.
- Live with a grateful heart. Being grateful for the things that you have will keep you in a flow of happiness and joy; which will bring you more of the good that life has to offer.

May you know God as your source and also stay connected to your source so that you may experience life more abundantly by getting all of your deepest desires fulfilled as you begin living life from within.